THE

SAVING

I NEED

THE
SAVING
I NEED

David Tensen
and Friends

POETRY CHAPEL
PRESS

Author website: www.davidtensen.com
Author email: david@davidtensen.com

Poetry Chapel Press
Brisbane, QLD, Australia

Cover Illustration: Copyright © 2021 David Tensen

Edited: Felicia Murrell
              www.yzcounsel.com

Also available in eBook and Audiobook format.

The Saving I Need / David Tensen. -- 1st ed.
ISBN 978-0-6489893-7-0

Dedicated to those

who refuse

to settle

on the

surface.

Table of Contents

Poetry Chapel Collective
Contributing Authors

Andrew Charles Adair

Abigail Bucks

Brian Bucks

Carly Caprio

Jessica Mussro

Jessica Stevens

Nicole Walker

Tineke Ziemer

INTRODUCTION

I've always been drawn to community... but I must confess: the older I get, the more selective I am with who I choose to spend time with. It's not for a lack of compassion or empathy for others, in fact, I think I hold more of both for people. I simply have less energy to spend on holding facades or guards up around those I feel unsafe or unsure around. It may be the cost of vulnerable living. Perhaps it is the cost of overdoing it in the past. Heck, it might just be a middle age thing - which explains why older people pay less attention to image management and people-pleasing.

Despite my apprehension, I'm so incredibly grateful I went with my gut and asked myself a simple question, 'What would it look like if you brought together relative strangers and journeyed for several months putting together a poetry collection?' I had enough poems of my own to publish another collection just fine, but I wondered if it were possible to foster a small writing community where we encourage and love on one another, sharing the sacraments of lives woven together in words.

The collection you hold in your hand is the result of this risky outreach. The weekly ZOOM gatherings across months, across time zones, across life events, across gender and age made for the kind of gathering many of us claimed was better than a Sunday service. Hardly a week went by without deep sighs, tears, laughter and *selah* moments as we broke open our lives, dreams and desires, penning them in poetic form. As the weeks grew, so did the vulnerability, skill and appreciation for this ancient form of communication. Thus, Poetry Chapel was born.

This book is made up of two halves. The first half is a collection of my poems. My last major collection *The Wrestle* exceeded my expectations of reach, sales and impact. Since its release, I have committed to writing as a service to the world, my faith and myself. As much as I hope you like my poems and they resonate with you, I lay them before you as an offering. Take. Eat. Or pass them by. The second half are poems the Poetry Chapel poets wrote and chose. Some were written during our time together. Other poems were pieces already written. Each poet was asked to provide a small bio. Each were given six pages to publish poems to. Personally, I think the collection is as beautiful as each poet. I couldn't be more proud. This much I know, you're sure to find a few poems worth bookmarking or taking a photo of for keepsake. Enjoy!

Much love,
David Tensen

On Divinity

Feeding God

His face
pressed against
her breast.

So, this
is what he looks like.
The one the prophets spoke of.
The one the angel offered.

Her eyes catch Joseph's
Mary whispers,
'He looks like us!'
'YHWH looks like us.'

His turned-up nose
now hunting for milk.
With trembling fingers
Mary does her best
to flick open the mouth of God

Pulling his head in
closer to her chest.
Closer to her heart.

In this way,
God receives his first meal.
In a stranger's home.
From the body
of a teenage Galilean.
Swallowing and slurping
like a hungry lamb.

The memory of every event
leading up to this moment
courses through her body.
Tears of relief
cross her olive cheeks
and fall upon her newborn.

As Joseph now
strokes her brow,
she closes her eyes,
looks up to the heavens,
and catches herself
giving thanks to God
who now lays in her arms.

Immanuel:
God
with
us.

The Chase

I didn't expect this
to be the kind of romance
where I pursue you
for a lifetime
and never come close
to possessing you.

Ironically,
that's what my religion
had me believe,
that I'd get you,
possess you
and harness you
by twisting your arm in prayer.
By holding you to words
scratched on scrolls
like you were subject
to some kind of caveat -
all the while
giving me hope
that I could mask
my worry and weakness
by winning a game
where even the most devoted
were found defeated.

But divine love
(I am discovering)
has no winners or losers.
Lovers don't race,
they chase.
They chase.
They chase
one another
through eternity's
narrow losses
and open gates
like crazy lovers
drunk on a dream
of all that will be
when they finally
find themselves.
Find themselves.
Find themselves
lost in union.

As If

little did I know
I was really looking
for a way to belong

so
I used you
and the book
others wrote of you
as a way to divide
the world
into camps
which always had me
at an advantage

us and them

in and out

clean and dirty

lost and found

winners and losers

as if
as if
as if your love
was partial
and the incarnation
was not enough
to hold it all

as if I
was not included
in the cosmos
you reconciled
into your selves

as if sin
and death
and my beliefs
were more powerful
than your passion

as if I
ever belonged
to any group
other than
loved
loved
loved
loved
loved

The Saving I Need

I used to cry out to you
For you
With fervour and volume
Not ceasing to bid
For divine intervention
Asking you to come
Like a rider of clouds
Like Deus Ex Machina
Like a warrior king

I'd petition you
To deliver me
And save me
From my suffering
From my lack
From my angst
And you did
You did
Till you didn't

It's like you stopped
Stopped allowing
Me to see you that way
Far away
Worlds away
Pushed away
So you delivered me
You saved me

Saved me from the lie
That you were distant
That you could leave me
Forsake me
Go against your word
Your nature
And be anywhere other
Than with me
Be anyone other
Than Immanuel

So I quit working
Quit striving
Allowing myself to rest
I took a break
From burnt offerings
Burning myself
Beating myself
And started loving myself
Like you do
I started learning
What it meant to be me
With you by my side
And it was great
Really great
Till it wasn't
And I needed saving again

You see
To know you are with me
Is a truth
And a joy
But a by-my-side
Best-friend-saviour
Way of knowing you
Still has me separate
Separate from union
Separate from oneness
Separate from discovering
My place in the divine dance
Which is where
You brought me
Eternally
Which is crazy
Which changes everything
But I'm learning
Slowly learning
That the truth of my being
My very being
Is you
You

Let's Doubt

Come, let's doubt together
Let's shout together
Let's make a mockery
Of absurd certainty
Let's doubt the evils of God
The false accounts of His retribution
Let's doubt that God is silent
And can't be heard in the darkness
Let's doubt that His open arms close
The moment hearts stop beating
Let's doubt our anxious imagination
Is mightier than His mercy
Let's doubt that God is bound
By 66 bound-up books
Let's doubt God's absence
May ever be discovered
Let's doubt separation from God
Is ever really possible
Let's doubt an abundance of evil
Can exhaust His boundless love
Let's doubt that God is partial
And piety buys us favour
Let's doubt that God has ever
Been troubled by our doubt

Questions and Doubts

I have questions
Lots of questions
Some are tough
Some I don't really want an answer to
And some are just sitting there
Finding refuge in the shadows
Waiting to be dressed in words.

Can I ask you, God?

I ask if I can ask
Because some questions
Might be mistaken for doubts
Or so I'm told
Like 'Why don't you heal everyone?'
Followed by 'Why did you make hell?'
And that's just a sample
And I'm a little hesitant
And those I asked
And those that preached
And those I looked up to
On pages and stages
Had me believing
That questions and doubts
Were naughty little neighbours
And I should be good
And do as they interpret

Not upset you
And just doubt my doubts instead
But...
I'm kinda doubting that now.

Can I ask you, God?

Because the way that I see it
I'm asking my dad
Whose always glad to see me
There's not been a time
Where you haven't been near
So I know when I speak
There's no doubt that you hear
And what child hasn't questions?
Isn't that how we grow?
Isn't that how we know
What you know?

Can I ask you, God?

I guess that's really my question.

Can I ask you, God?

Cast Upon Waters

The mystery of my being
Swallowed up by Christ
Is to me like a loaf of bread
Broken
        in this life
        by this life
Into many, many pieces.

Each portion then
Cast upon waters.
Some cast by question
Some by surrender
Some by devotion
Much by angst
Most unknowingly.

Of the bread which returns
I've learnt
To throw it back
To sow it back
To the sea
Until it is soaked
And descends -
Dancing in circles
With the current
Like wild broken lovers
To the ocean floor.
To the ground
        of being.

A Hanging Request

I love how you healed wounds
yet chose to wear yours
and still do to this day
as a reminder
to the Trinity
and principalities
of your solidarity
with all humanity
with all that is in me
and eternally marked
by the oppression of systems
which you gave yourself to
right down
to a hanging request
for those blinded
with power,
"Father, forgive them,
for they don't know
what they are doing."

Harrowing Hell

Into the darkness
You descended
accommodating
every unimaginable atrocity.
Eliminating
every lie we can conjure
that Your boundless mercy
has bounds
and you would dare
leave it to the living
to share Good News.
Personally,
you took the hand
of the wretched and damned -
every part of us
we've shamed
out of view
but not from You -
assuring creation
that Love
will harrow hell
if that's what it takes
to be one.
If that's
what it takes
to be one.

Thank You, Fire

Thank you, Fire
Found in co-suffering
Found in love
Found in failing
Found in being loved.

Thank you, Fire
Present this side of the veil
Present this very day
Present this valley of shadows
Present this resurrected life

Thank you, Fire
Flames you endured
Flames you live in
Flames you refine with
Flames upon my head

Fire.
We welcome you, Fire.
The life you leave, Fire.
Burn away the stubble and hay, Fire.
May we learn to respond in ways
that bring warmth, not scarring, Fire.

Strangers and Friends

Close Friends

You may be
the rarest of souls
blessed enough
to have close friends.

And I hesitate
to pluralise the word friend
because to have
just one close friend
is an incomparable
and abundant gift.

And I hesitate
to use the word close
because fair-weather friends
who fail to share umbrellas
or refuse to hold hands
in lightning storms
don't count as close -
to me, anyway.

No, I'm talking about
a friend
(two at most)
so close and committed to you
you'd swear on the other's life
with heaven as your witness
the feeling between you,
forged over years,
is mutual.

Strangers

A prayer for my children

I pray you never take
the kindness of a stranger
for granted -
knowing their gestures
are open invitations
to see them
as sisters, brothers
and friends, at least.
Further,
I pray you would strive
to be known
by those names, daily.

Whispers and Yell

Perhaps you should ignore them -
  those that yell directions
    from the stands.
Never setting a sole on the soil
  that stains your feet.
Never getting to gaze through the eyes
  you rub clear every morning.
Never hearing the heart
  that beats to the rhythm
    of your life,
      not theirs.
Pay them no mind.
Save your attention
  for the upward call
    and the incarnational One
      who knows your name
      and doesn't yell,
        but whispers it -
          breathing fire into your bones.

Lashes

Oh
how I wish you would think more
or
at least break bread
with those you chastise
so
you could stare into their eyes
and they into yours
till
one of you blinks
or fails to see God between lashes

Endless Chances

Peter failed many times
But you never sent him out
He, like me, punished himself
For lacking commitment
For lacking foresight
For betting on his own wits
To hold things together
Not knowing you first loved us
And will last love us
With a love that lasts
Beyond a rooster crowing
Which I'm sure was as common
As the notifications I get
Asking me where I am
Why I'm late
Why I lost
And that I'm loved
And forgiven
And allowed to be human
Because God knows
Really knows
How to sit by a fire
And serve a meal
Of endless chances
To remind me
That we are simply fishing
And not playing chess for keeps.

Generous Friends

Blessed
beyond measure
is the one found planted
in a field among generous friends.
Like great oaks, every act of kindness
sown to the soil strengthens the forest floor,
their nourishing
roots
grafting
as
one
to
weather every season's storm.

Home and Away

The Warriors Return

Welcome home
the weary warrior.

Do not shame their failings,
for they mark valiant efforts.

Do not pity their wounds,
for they mark many wars.

The return offers them
a barter and a trade:
  Straight arrows for bent answers.
  Sharp sword for smouldering sage.
  Youthful courage for aged concern.

Bless now, the movement
from warrior to elder,
for this is the task
of the tribe.

Bless their triumphs
and bless their tragedies,
for they bud from
the same branch.

Bless their works
and bless their wounds,
for they are both
born in the battle.

And
Bless their frame
and bless their frailty
for they are
both home
to God.

At Path's End

the end of a path
need not be
the end of the walk
even if you turn to return
your eyes
and the world
grant you
a new perspective
a new knowing
where the trees dance
and the birds sing
to a new song
the moment has brought you
so, walk.
walk and discover
a new world
on the old path
home

Blast Off

Blast off the last failure
Like it's a platform
To the dark space
   of new beginnings.

Starting from the ground up
Make a sound
Shake the ground
Cover the shrinking
     spectators in billows
       of dust, smoke and
      forgiveness.

But most of all
    scream for joy;
you are on your way
   to being
     weightless.

Give Tomorrow a Break

I may give tomorrow a break
Leave it on the other side of the sun
It will come around when it's ready
It always does

Problems cannot pass through planets
Stress cannot shoot down stars
How could concern correct tomorrow's course?
It simply can't

So I may give tomorrow a break
Postpone till it peeks over my pillow
Welcome any worries that wake up
And tag them for today

The Call

I made the mistake
of believing the call
would come
without chaos or loss.
But now I can see
this far down the road
that nothing is gained
without cost.

Do not be deceived
the call is no thing
to embark on
void of decision.
Find me just one
who has done it fear-free
and I'll show you
the one without vision.

Because if you think
a win or a loss
all depends
on you reaching a goal,
you've missed the whole point
of a call, don't you see?
It's about being true
to your soul.

Moving On

Cracks

it's the cracks
on the road to wholeness
you have to watch for

the novice avoids them,
scuttling with speed
across the bitumen

hoping to reach
a promised land
without tripping

but the wise slow down
knowing the road
has no end

the wise have learnt
the cracks are
the way forward

going down
into the narrows
where seeds fall

tending to a garden
once lost
in the shadows

discovering
the road is a cover
and a keeper

the cracks are a door
and wholeness
is found in the dirt

Forget Not

forget not the seeds
you sowed
in your toil
as your brow dripped
blood red

forget not the wells
you dug
in the desert
as the stranger's water
gave strength

forget not the valleys
you illuminated
in your seeking
as darkness gave way
to your shadow

Thickets

Just beyond yourself,
Beyond the thicket
And bracken
Of broken hope,
Tiredness and trauma
Lives a version of you
Who knows what it's like
To have marched
Through it all.

Not perfectly,
Or without a scratch.
But definitely.

Go now.
Greet them.
Grab their hand
And don't let go.
It's where you need to be.

(After David Whyte)

Your Happiness

You must be careful
On who gets a say
In your happiness

There are too many voices
Pushing their choices
With one goal in mind

To make you believe
Their voice is yours

And before you know it
You've made them happy
At your own expense

For the Courageous Creators

Consider carefully
the weight you give
to those
whose only contribution
to all things
well intentioned and beautiful
is a cutting comment.

Consider their hands,
clean of paint,
stains,
or the joyful strain
of making something
multiplied
from your soul's infinite desire
to express itself through art.

Consider those cutting comments
as nothing more than a sign
that you are simply one
who has chosen a path
of making over taking
delivery over destruction
creation over criticism
and life over death.

That Flame

Hold that flame real tight.
It has been in you
flickering and flailing
in unison with limbs
ever since you sparked
in your mother's womb.

Shield your flame
from the winds
of criticism, conformity
and shame.
Do not sell it
or think it will stay lit
in the hands of another.

Never forget:
your flame
will never scorch you -
but to keep it dancing
may be painful
and costly at times.

So,
hold your own flame close.
Attend to your own genius.
Walk your own path.
Foster your divine gift.

And may you
one day,
for many days,
find a tribe of elders
who bless you enough
that your flame fans
and shines so bright
it sets all of creation
alight.

Hold On, Dear One

Hold on, dear one, life is
for you, even when
it is hidden behind
fear's hands, or beneath
pain's blanket, or beyond
sorrow's darkly stained sight,
life is for you.

Hold on, dear one, not because
life is too much, or because
you are too much, but because
life is beautiful, and in
your eyes and touch, and
every blinking breath, life
in you is beautiful.

Hold on, dear one, life is
in you, and worth holding
on to, and worth holding
loosely but never letting
go of, as life holds on
and on, and on
and on to you.

Just You Wait

a newborn cannot
string a sentence together.
does that bother you?

seeds must disappear
into the earth before bouquets bloom.
is that ok?

every overnight success
followed endless nights of nothing.
did anyone tell you that?

life leads to death,
death to resurrection.
for eons the cosmos held classes on this.

give that new thing time.

allow it to disappear in the dirt for a season.

know that restless nights are normal.

and death is not the closing scene.

Sway

I'm learning to sway   more gently now.
Bearing weight   on one leg
then the other.   On strengths,
then limitations.   Giving each
the time they need.   And with intent
I find myself   walking.

On Me

More Times So Kind

You've had your way with me
More times than I can count
More times than I can speak of
More times so kind
That only poets and angels
Dare use words to describe

Like that time you held me
As a wounded warrior
Tight against your chest
Close against your heart
For what felt like years
Like a father who understood
Like a mother who fell asleep
Nursing her sick child

Like that time you met me
In that shameful memory
And instead of getting angry
You put your hand on my shoulder
And shone your face upon me
Like a father who blesses
Like a mother who smiles away
Her child's fears

Like that time you waited with me
By that bus stop
After they'd finished with me
And you sat on the curb
Hurt and crying with me
Like a father who'd been there
Like a mother who heals
With just two words:
Oh, Darling

And now I have just two words:
Thank you
No, just one word.
Stay.

This Much I Know

This much I know -
that rainbow rays
depend on how
I gently hold
the diamond of a day
against the spinning sun
or waxing moon.

And I know
that mountains
I make from molehills
can't be moved
despite my strength
or mustard seed faith

And I know
that finding God
in a snowflake
still melts at my molding
dripping through my hand
into a form of its own choosing

And so today
I remind myself
that before I close my eyes
I can be sure
that tomorrow they will meet
colours,
molehills
and snowflakes
no man has seen before.
This much
I know.

Forty-Three

It has taken time,
decades, in fact
to call myself beloved
and settle into this body -
even as parts wear
and blurry eyes demand
I step back
to see the bigger picture.

I have the world to be grateful for,
parents who care deeply,
the love of family
friends
and strangers
who serve me with their peace,
children who still wear
my arm as a scarf
when we walk together -
they, more than anyone else
bear my flaws,
fair skin and curiosity.

I will not lie.
this life and its bright frailty
weigh heavy on me.
I want nothing more
than to leave one day
far from now
having tread light enough
and shone bright enough
that one day
my name may fall
from the mouth of an ancestor
(or perhaps a stranger)
in a kind and generous way.

The Prisoner

I've ignored you
locked you up
only letting you out
when needed
pain forged cell bars
made to last
made for darkness
made of lies

in me
(the mansion)
you sat deep
out of sight
out of mind
a shameful prisoner
whose cries echoed
in times of silence
through the chambers
of my heart

I still remember
when I braved the silence
and the darkness
and the descent
to visit you
to sit and listen
because your cries
were so loud
I could no longer afford
to ignore you
to ignore me

we sat silent
for so long
both knowing
truth and confession
were our only way
out of the darkness

eventually you spoke
spoke of things
only by grace
and patience
and exhaustion
I was ready to hear

we both wept
we both knew
our world would differ
things would change

the harmonious ascent
was new
considering one another
walking lockstep
as a march of freedom
to the sound of healing
to the cadence of a new verse
to the song of salvation
to
the
truth
that no part of me
should ever be a prisoner again.

Trauma is a Weaver

Trauma is a weaver
And I
And I am a masterpiece
Entwined over time
With ancestors divine
This body I call mine
And every cell
That tells a story
Is a majestic tapestry
Of meaning and miracles
Holy in every sense
Unfolding and blooming
Revealing truth to me
That thorn threaded crowns
Are at home
In God's brow -
And this same God is not
Ashamed
Exempt
Or far
From that which leaves a scar
And neither am I.

My Present Concern

I do wonder more often
Now they are teens
How my children will
Live in a land and economy
Governed and priced in such a way
That the long swim
to the great Australian Dream
Starts under water
In debt-soaked, heavy clothes
Towards an unsustainable horizon
Inhabited and ruled by generations
Who live for their long day
Seemingly unaware
That wages haven't moved
In decades
But increased living costs
Only serve to push
The dream
Further out of reach.

My daughter and her friends
Now talk of tiny homes
Shared blocks
And mobile lifestyles
As their world increases
Job certainty decreases
And they hear stories
Of how grandpa's humble wage
Was enough to appease
Bank managers
Who loaned a dollar
Backed by gold
And not watered down
By printing billions -
Which was once called fraud
But now goes by quantitative easing.

And my concerns increase
Along with arguments
Among the uninformed
And selectivity blind voices
Whose age privileges them
The gift to dismiss
The declining health of a planet
They will be buried in
Before long.
But it matters to my children
And so, it matters to me
So I can't wait
Till they hold seats
In parliament and policy
And make tough decisions too.
Which I can only pray
Considers all creation
Swimming in their gentle wake.

Inner and Outer

Landscapes

I Will Not Become Fear

Though I may fear
I will not become fear

Though its overwhelming presence
has made its way
into the fabric of my soul,
I will not allow it to possess me.
I will not become fear.

May the sound of my voice
and the water from my eyes
be found in the songs and streams
with those who long for deliverance.
I will not become fear.

I will not walk perfectly
but I pray I will tread
with care and compassion.
Oppressive empires may not like it,
but what's new?
I will not become fear.

May the sick, lame, hungry,
oppressed and enslaved,
the traumatised, lost
bankrupt and broken
remain on the horizon of my heart
and my prayers.
I will not become fear.

Piss Off, Perfection

Compassion heard my story.
The whole thing.
Thought the reason was valid.
Called me beautiful
and told me she was there for me.

Perfection heard my story.
Some of it.
Thought it was another excuse.
Called me a victim
and told me I must climb up to be with her.

Piss off, Perfection

On Blowing Shame's Cover

Shame speaks with terrible accuracy
With a voice so convincing
You'll think it's your own
With timing so good
You'll swear that it knows
How you move
And breathe
And have your being

Shame has a way of tailing you
Lurking in the shadows
Like a malicious spy
Ready to arrest you
Tearing you away
From the truth
That you are
And will always be
enough

Shame conquers like mold
And before you know it
You're echoing its lies
Lies of lovers
Lies of strangers
Lies of you
And it's about time
that it ends...

Shame is not hard to find
Just listen for the 'I ams'
And the 'You ares'
And the 'People say'
Pay attention to
The sinking feelings
And shrinking feelings
And closed-in ceilings
And if it's not loving
Gracious, spacious
Or humane
You'll know
It's worth ignoring
And then exploring
The divine truth
Of your magnificent place
In all things

Miracles

I believe in all kinds of miracles.
The ones performed in a moment
where prayers pierce heaven
and suffering ceases in seconds.
Also, the most spectacular ones
where pain is managed across a lifetime
and love endures despite loss.

Earth Wounds

And there were those who dared
To look beyond their years
To the weeping of the ice caps
And forests being cleared.

They braved against the urge
Of doing as they pleased
Without a second thought
For the world they'd one day leave.

There rose a generation
Who heard creation moan
They traded dreams of mansions
For simpler, smaller homes.

They learnt to live with less.
Were mindful how they ate.
Worked hard to build a future
For their planet's sake.

And as they let their love
For all creation rise
They tended to the earth-wounds
Their parents left behind.

Dear Anxiety

Perhaps you've been
And may always
Be
In our midst
Like a breathtaking
Moment
Like a startling
Event
Like a shared
Dreaming
Like a shaky
Pavement
Like a swirling
Room

You start wars
And avoid them
You fuel fires
And quench them
Your unreasonable rule
Demands attention
Ignores ignorance
And spreads
From those
Who refuse
To acknowledge
Your name
Your presence
Your pointing out
Of cracks
In our
Collective soul

Anxiety,
I see you.

SECTION 2

The Poetry Chapel Collective
Chosen Works

Andrew Charles Adair

I was born in Sydney, Australia, in 1961 and spent most of my early childhood exploring its eastern coastline. I longed to recall the wonder of these adventures by the sea and trained my imagination to recall and reflect their beauty in the chosen medium of writing. Teachers also encouraged me to build expressive muscles, and their influence culminated in some success.

The passion to write continued strongly and became a vocational focus until I immersed it, to the great surprise of friends and family, into a newly recovered faith in 1982. Writing then became sporadic and secondary. I became involved in a lot of diverse works. Looking after the homeless in our block of flats, a Christian twelve step recovery program, and a year with a Messianic Jewish congregation to name a few.

I met my wife Victoria in the late 90s. Daring adventures ensued. We ran a Crisis accommodation centre, took up senior leadership in a church on the NSW (New South Wales) South Coast, and then went deep into the heart of East Africa to study community missions with Heidi and Rolland Baker of IRIS Global.

My poems are eclectic views of the beauty of redemptive love, the miracle of the mingling of Divine and human Presence, and finding healing in liminal marginal places. Some reflect academic reading as well as mystical encounters which I try to present as bread for everyone to discover and enjoy.

You can find my poems on Instagram: @avadair

Hibernation

Amongst the red stones of Scotland
resting innocence in the Celtic hearth,
A cupboard escape, eternal secret place
stay here while we search for our nests
as the soil turns over in our hearts.

Sun descending to the solstice summit
hand of time seeming faster in afternoons
We are waiting for sabbatical sleep
tenured spirits in heaven's emerald peace

Regenerate the loams of bitter ages
crunch to powder thorn and thistle
We want the sleep of life
the rest of resurrection resolved

We want seasons beyond the dark tunnel of life
tidal rhythms in seas of fiery glass
Hardened eternal attributes stand fast
as the soil turns over in our hearts

Throne and love-seat where lion and lamb rest
together in nativity and sonship
all resolved anger blessed.
Our rest and atmosphere's air
Can we hibernate until we get there?

Covid Kangaroos

Hibernating in the twilight
before the onset of a siesta
between the nod off
and the dream,
drip fed with melatonin
brought on by
blinking sunlight
on amber April afternoons

I long to be with this mob
in a field
laying low
never having to frame a question
contemplating
rested workdays
bush tucker
surveillance
and play

In a matter of weeks
city traffic will scream
adrenalin for melatonin
drowsy autumn
will leave us
shuddering in winter

Let the dust of sleep hide me
momentarily
from role, rhyme and reason.

Weeping for Hemingway

I wept for Hemingway
as his foot reached trauma's shore
I wept for the uneasy return he had
myth decaying
I wept
He was swept far
too far from shore

Writers should travel far out, you said
Pen, paper and war-torn soul
in unmanageable currents
swirling eddies
uncertainties
things which I too have
sought to report
things far
so far from shore

What is the scoop
from these gulfstream trenches?
Is our masculinity fading
Graceful danger not so satisfying?
Revive rites of passage
REVIVE!
Will you tell of
a black marlin leaping,
line stressed to breaking
small skiff gliding
and sliding alone.
Will you haul and hold him
as sharks circle to spoil him?

O mourn these bleached bones
left for scholars
and tourists
to find!

I carried my own father on my back
up the stairs to his bedroom to convalesce
Hauling in and holding him
before a final stop was made
sharks circled
not much was left

An ambulance retrieved him
in a Scottish hospital
Papa was laid to rest

Wild currents swirled in the passage threshold
A baton passed by
 I reached out to hold.

Blackened Universe

Uni-verse
One script and symphony
myriad songs sustaining
harmonies and frequencies limitless
arranging, growing and fading
your melodies we hear as laws
mirroring immortality.

We set you on fire!
Sorry, Blessed creation!
In countenance loud we torched you!
Proud flinty tongues clashed
Wildfire ensued
Interest compounded
Pyro-cumulus whirlwinds crossed the land.

Now we speak peace to you
May you terraform under grace
an earth that responds.
Warm us safely
unreflective of our anger.
Let cherub clouds frame renaissance skies.

I struggle with your shadow self,
Armoured apex guardian.
Wild fanged predator.
Are you trysting with us in mutual rape?
My shadow with your shadow?
In the embrace you whisper
that you need
Redemption.

Redemption like us.
And like us,
affirmation.

Affirmation
and kind kisses.

We are ready to accept this dance now
our cupboards grow bare.

We are family.
You are our earth.
You are our skies.
We both, hopeful portals of dust
 respect the Light
entering our frames.
Light that creates anew.

Beyond
mysterious shining highways
linking galaxies
sings us both
across the threshold.

New heavens
marrying,
carrying
a new bride
home.

Abigail Bucks

My name is Abigail (Abby) Bucks. For me, home is back at the farm in Mitchell, Nebraska, with family.

Currently, I'm out of state at university studying history and political science with plans to graduate May 2022, with my bachelors.

I have an avid love for learning and helping others learn and hope to become a professor someday. When I'm not taking pen to paper, my nose can often be found in a book. I also have an immense love for turtles, plants, and typewriters.

Poetry has been a way for me to find expression, as well as a medium for me to work through depression, anxiety, and chronic illness, particularly in a way that has brought me close to God. In addition to poetry, I love writing fiction novels.

This poetry collective has been a wonderful blessing for me to branch out in new ways and gain confidence in sharing my poetry.

Jars

Love is not
A mason jar

Left to sit on
Tables & desks

Forgotten in old
Cabinets & cupboards.

Love is not
A bell jar

To lock you inside
Glass walls

Nor is it to be
A scientific classification.

Love is not
A cookie jar

Holding sweet goodness
Only distributed after dinner

Not used as
Punishment or reward.

Love is not
A killing jar

A trap you get
Caught inside

Leaving you a specimen
Observed as inhuman.

All in
A l l:

Love is not
A glass jar

It does not know
Encased limitations

Nor so fragile to easily shatter when
D r o p p e d.

Growth

Stuck.
I am
Stuck.
Stagnant,
In this place.
And I can't remember
how to grow.
How do I grow?

The thing is:
Like a
Sapling,
I don't think I'm supposed
To do
Anything
At
All...
Except
Soak,
In water,
In sun.
I only need
To be
A little
Tree.
But it's hard
Because:
I don't S E E the growth.
Why don't I FEEL the growth?

It's hard to want to grow,
So much faster,
Than you are.
Because you can't
"REMEMBER"
How to grow.
        You just do.

And by oversoaking,
In water,
You DROWN.
And by oversitting,
In the sun,
You B U R N.
You can't force your roots,
To go deep
        & DOWN.
That is not how growing works.

I wish I could have
Learned this much sooner:
You can't "REMEMBER"
How to grow.
You just do.
You
Just
Grow.

Fragments

You don't
have to
fix everything.

All the broken pieces,
even if they were
caused by you,
don't
belong
to
you.

All the broken pieces,
the ones that
make up you,
are not
meant to
be patched
together
with
glue.

All the broken pieces,
of everything
all around you,
are not meant to be
collected
& carried
as you fruitlessly
attempt to make things
"good as new."

The pieces
of these things
which you hold
so desperately,
will
only
cut
you.

You don't have to fix
yourself.
You don't have to fix
others.
You don't have to fix
the world.
You will only bleed
blue.

Leave
those fragments on the floor
For God to collect
and put back together,
as He
knows how to
infuse
all the broken pieces
with gold
and love.
To fix everything
for you.

Brian Bucks

I am married and we are Christ followers. We have lived on the western edge of Nebraska for the past thirty-four years and have three adult children. From our small horse farm, we have a distant view of Laramie Peak in Wyoming.

What captures me with poetry is the expression of the complexity of being human stripped to a raw form. Courage is required at times to wrestle and speak clearly about topics we as a society tend to avoid. These uncomfortable topics languish on the periphery of life and cause great harm to the soul. Courage and vulnerability are important and deserve a voice that poetry provides.

Among my eclectic interests are Border Collies, Australian Shepherds and herding dogs; photography; writing; and teaching. I have a degree in mechanical engineering and work in substation automation, control, and protection.

You can see more of my writings at http://westernnebraskapoet.blogspot.com or on Instagram: @highplainspoet. My most recent book, At the Edge, can be found on Amazon.

Baptism

Carrying truth...

in an open bucket
filled to the top

sloshing about

the jeans
are going to
get wet

oh, how that wet denim
sticks greedily, like Velcro
on pale, cold flesh

Meanwhile...

truth and shame,
don't mix well

they leave bitterness
upon the tongue

life's flotsam in that bucket
like last year's rotting leaves

trying to dissect the debris
as if trying to atone my own sin –
...sigh...

it just doesn't work,
it only muddies the water more
so, pour out that brackish mixture
in the light,
without shame,
kneeling on the ground,
examine the offering

rinse out that bucket,
scrub it clean
then fill it to the rim
with truth once again

Somehow...

it's lighter, free of shame and regret
as it sloshes about
truth, now just feels wet

God Of

You are the God
Of
All...
All that was
And
All that wasn't

You are the God
Who
Draws...
Draws me close
And
Launches me out

You are the God
Who
Takes...
Takes my brokenness
And
Transforms it into beauty

You are the God
Who
Asks...
Asks me to step out
Without
Google maps to guide me

You are the God
Who
Is...
Is with me
Inviting me to join
With You

You are the God
Who
Passionately...
Passionately pursues me
Relentlessly
Woos me

You are the God
Who
I ask...
Ask do I see me
As You see me?

Like a Turtle

My daughter loves sea turtles.
And like a turtle
    in life's current she flows
and "no-matter" how far she goes
    she always carries her home

Finding sandy shores
    then plunging into the surf again
in fresh exploration she goes
    yet, drawn back to her bale

Touchpoint of family
    where she comes out of her shell
washed in waves of renewing love
    summoned to see again
        summoned to sea, she goes
      knowing all is well

Before I Close My Eyes

Just before I close my eyes
I wash away all the shame
like the stains on my knees
remembering I am Your child

I took a tumble while grasping for love
stumbling forward I'm learning love,
like walking,
is controlled falling

I imagine the smile creasing your lips
and the twinkle in Your eyes,
your Father's joy in my new steps
as I'm wrapped in your tender arms

This is what I imagine tonight
just before I close my eyes

Carly Caprio

I grew up in Colorado thinking my body was void of creative bones. I thought I was tone deaf; I hated piano classes, drew stick figures, and would choose P.E. over art any day.

As I began the journey of seeking something bigger than myself, I relocated to South America before moving to New York City. It was here I finally outran myself and was left to face years of hidden grief, longings, fears, and harms done to others. Right on time, poetry found me on a subway I'd ridden a dozen times before. I don't remember what it said but I liked the sound of it.

Writing began as an outlet to pull out what was buried deep within, that which threatened to drive me (and others around me) mad. These poems reflect a difficult and necessary chapter in my life. I never thought they were any good nor did I ever imagine publishing them. Slowly, poetry has become an oasis to share how I see the world and appreciate the way others do.

Now I find myself in a collective with talented poets beyond my understanding. I wonder, "How did this happen?" I don't know and I don't ask for fear of waking from a pleasant dream.

It's been quite the plot twist for a Colorado girl who grew up believing creativity was not in her cards. My hope is my poems touch one or two of you along the way. Thanks for reading.

Fallen Love

Like a couple of trees
our leaves brushed
elbows, flirting
wind whipped through
our willows, teasing
our trunks twisted
together, fiery.

Wrinkles now bark
the corners of your eyes
I see them when I look at you
lost is where love
used to smile back
now. . .pain, loss, regret.

Fallen trees
find purpose
in bridging banks
back together,
so, too,
is how I carry hope
for you.

Cascades

Your tears
cascade into rivers
carving canyons
through your skin
where your broken heart
finds its way
home.

Me too.

Grief

All this grief
of what was, what isn't,
and what could have been.

Grief of clenched fists
clasping stolen desires,
old tricks,
and expired chaos,
the kind that cuts
through the nose
like rotting beauty.

Grief of her soul parting too soon,
leaving missing heartbeats
behind as once warm embraces
evaporate in the waking presence
of a meaningful absence.

Grief of letting myself feel it
and all the years I didn't,
of what's to come
and what's still left,
of the hair I lost,
the tan that faded,
and shortening summer sunsets
making room for
undressing autumn trees.
How generous.

Grief of the man who loved me
and the careless love I claimed for him,
Of the actions I took and
the way I wish
  Oh, how I wish
I had taken different ones.

Sobering is a reality demanding grief,
one that leaves no out
but through. . .
A truth
 that also
must be
grieved.

Comparison

You help us makes sense
of
how different boats
navigate a single storm
And yet,
you lie to our longings
as we lust for sails
not meant to move us.

You reveal beauty
of colliding cultures
on land masses of green and blue
dance, danza, danse.
And yet,
you rob us
of the beauty
of unfolding
the life we are selected to live
(as if it wasn't a privilege).

You lock our eyes on the lives
we were only meant to
be inspired by.

You teach us lessons
of
lamenting with stories
whose origins we do not share.
And yet,
our tears drop in vain
as you place our pain
on hierarchies of perceptions.

Quietly, you hiss the lie:
the only way
to make sense
of this world
is to make
them
less than
us
or
us
less than
them.

You beautiful thief.

Kara Chidlow

I share a home in Western Australia with my husband and two cheeky sons.

I am a Registered Nurse currently studying Art Therapy. In the windows that mothering affords, you will find me working on a growing number of incomplete painting projects or in good company drinking too much tea.

To be honest, writing poetry first started from a place of jealousy. My husband inspired me to start! It was a tool that enabled us to process and articulate deep pain through a trying time.

I have always considered myself not the 'creative' type. Though with every poem written, that lie grows quieter. On this joyous journey, thus far, I've learnt creativity seems to flow more from a place of surrender than striving.

Alice Walker once said,

"Whenever you are
creating beauty around
you, you are restoring
your own soul."

Being a part of this poetry collective has indeed been soul restoring. I pray my poems inspire you to fasten your heart to hope and pursue inner transformation.

Journey with me on Instagram: @creativechasey

Petition

Begin below
Be ignored of men
Adopt the way of
self-forgetfulness
Drop pen

Stoop low
Humility, He calls
Beckoning you to
energetically
Cast to the wind
hubris and
obsequious modesty

Heed the maxim,
pride proceeds a fall
Deny prides entry
Nursing its sorrows,
sullen and sulky
It obsesses with
things peripheral

With a hand of prayer
And a hand of faith
Wrap around yourself,
a servant's apron
Like a backwards cape,
this smock will help you
fly above the frons

Master, master
Who shall do most to oblige
and profit all the rest?
Is that life's question,
if not its test?

Subtle

Sometimes
bravery
whispers.
Up the walls,
alley's,
corridors,
down the halls.
Her acts
unwitnessed,
though they are.

Blushing.
Brittle.
Bravery.

You are
applauded
no matter
how small, tall,
tender, or
tough on the
exterior.

Bravery comes
in bottles
of fragrances
both heady,
and with notes
of subtlety.

Do you
recognise
her scent
when she
passes
by?

Trenched

Laying side by side.
Human khaki carpet,
galvanized to life
by the trumpet's sound.

The realisation hits,
we are heading to
the frontline pew.

Cesspools of boredom
interrupted by
bursts of terrors,
that chafe
and weep with time.
Lice-infested,
life in the trenches.

Hundreds and thousands
of men, mutinied
by authorities'
decrees and directives.
Maintaining morale
is a must, but how?

Trench art.
Isn't that what we are
creating here?
Taking
battlefield debris and
turning it into
art or poetry.

These are the flares
that uncover the
enemy, prowling
for prey unawares.

And when the match is
in the powder barrel,
propel the flare and
grenade grace grants. Then
pray to see the angels
amongst the ashes,
aiding the injured.

Secure the vestige
of faith amongst you.
Until the Lieutenant
lowers the ladder,
it is going to be a
lengthy, ludicrous
war of wills.

Nicole Fisher

Since I can remember, I have been curious about people, life and how it all fits together. I was a shy kid, an overthinker by day and vivid dreamer by night, but it was Sunday school that planted seeds of faith and deeper meaning. I am one for nostalgia with a love of things from yesteryear and can get lost in people's stories and memories. Creative expression is now a daily necessity and nature helps me quiet my busy mind. I previously carried unresolved grief, trauma and was suffocating in survival mode with nowhere for my emotions to go. I returned to writing. It was like turning on a tap with a flood of feelings, bringing release and joy helping my healing and faith journey. I now try to find beauty and hope even during the darker uncertain seasons of life.

Being part of The Poetry Collective has been an unexpected yet timely gift that I will treasure. It has encouraged me to delve deeper and embrace my truths as they are and set them free - imperfect and raw.

I have never considered myself a writer or poet, and yet I am here, and I am proud to be nestled amongst these pages with incredible humans and with you. Thank you for taking the time to connect with us. May your heart be encouraged to keep asking questions as you uncover and discover more than you ever imagined.

Originally from the Hunter Valley NSW, I now reside in Queensland, Australia, with my husband and son.

You can read more of my poetry on Instagram: @n.e.fisher.poetry

Alight

By the light
Of your candle
Nostalgic romantic

By the light
Of your phone
Intrusive addictive

Modern day forbidden fruit
Glutinous gigabytes
Plethora of information

Hard to find the truth
How do you see in the dark
Shadows in front or behind

Waiting to pluck you out
Plunge you deeper
Delay your journey

Artificial light
Cold and controlled
Imitating what you desire

Pause
Listen
Look

Find a flint, light the fire
Flames now dancing in the dark
Comfort for the heart

Here now, instant
Eyes red, tired, dim
Can everything be illuminated again

By the light of the moon
Escaping unnatural tombs
Carved out of digital disease

A plague we couldn't see
Arrives in a shiny new box
A cost greater than gold

Did you sell your soul
For this generic mould
An additional limb

Felt when missing
By the light of the fire
Sounds better to me

Beware of this tiny device
Its seemingly innocent
presence in your life

Face to screen last thing I see
Until I wake beside my lifeless friend
Charged hours we will spend

Making memories or wasting time
Don't let it hide your beautiful face
Your limitless mind

Will we be buried together
Discovered 200 years later
Human remains tied to machines

Unplug
Leave it behind
Sometimes

While the sun still

Burns bright

Nearer or Farther

Fathered
Fatherless

One or the other
None the less

A Father's Love
Warm embrace, unashamed, giving time
Endless grace, willing you to win your race

A l w a y s

A Father's Hate
Slap to your face, generational pain, feelings of
shame Scars keeping you silent, hidden away

B l a m e

An Absent Father
Left, unknown, untraced, separate lives, lost stories
Living elsewhere, unaware, alternate family

O b l i v i o u s

A Working Father
Incessantly making money night and day
Managing numbers, buying your love in place of
time

U n s e e n

A Lost Father
Lacking, drifting, absentminded, can't communicate
Entranced by hurts, addictive distractions

N u m b

A Mother Turned Father
Can do as you could not
Empowered, resilient, endless efforts

G r a t e f u l

A Dead Father
Silent, material reminders, lingering presence
Heartbroken. Memories alive in photos past

M i s s e d

A Stepfather
Restorative, trying his best, blended families
Kindness shared and bared through seasons

F r i e n d s

A Grieving Father
Never to hold you again, arms aching
Determined to keep his memories revived

L o n g i n g

An Adoptive Father
Seeking and wanting you as his own
Kin bonded bloodlines, family trees grow and bloom

H o p e

An Eternal Father
Before and after. Undeniable love
Almighty and just. Welcomes you home

A l w a y s

Chenonetta Jubata

Ducks in a row
I never liked that phrase
I saw twenty ducks
On twenty posts at the lake
Standing to attention
Waiting for their next direction

Ducks in a row
What does that mean?
I wonder once more
As I see one duck, standing on one post
Looking at me, I drive past in slow-motion
Eyes meeting on my morning commute

Ducks in a row
Ducks not hunted or stuffed
Ducks not cooked or hanging from hooks
Ducks not worn or laid upon
Ducks wading and waddling
Tending to young or just being one

Ducks in a row
Ducks flying high in V formation
Any direction, any occasion
Changing shape
Changing speed
Changing altitude as they need

This is how I like my ducks to be: Free

Scroll on

Afraid of the ordinary
Avoiding popularity
When did all my friends become ads
Encouraging a better life
Like the one they have
Promoting gimmicks and fads
Mostly unpaid for all the hashtags
A few freebies thrown into a gift bag
Growing younger, spending more
On things that don't really matter at all
Buy and spend
Waste, don't mend
Buy new not old
Keep feeding the beast
It's easy to please
In a mirage of success
Just keep playing to impress
Fake it till you make it
Dancing in fancy dress

...I digress
When did real life end, did it even begin?
Fake new clones becoming on trend
Perfect smiles, families framed in tiny boxes
Happiness reduced to likes
When did you lose your sense of self?
Once genuine, no filtered faces
Scrolling
Scrolling
Scroll on
Will you find
what you are looking for?

Matthew Hardy

I was born in the early 90's, in Newcastle, Australia. Growing up in a small-town church and school, I was immersed in a community that had a focus on family.

Inspired by a leader, sibling, and teacher in my early teens, I became a lover of music and song writing. Although I struggled in English throughout my schooling, I stumbled onto poetry through my song writing.

After high school I felt drawn to another community church in Byron Bay. With this change came a focus to the importance of the heart, healing, relationships and communication. I found myself through this shift to the heart, and through studying counselling.

From this journey I have gained a passion to write on things of the heart and the knowledge that can be found from love.

This short collection of poems comes from part of my journey. They have helped me process, voice tension and find resolve.

I hope they speak to you.

I pray they bless you!

A Lover of Humanity

What is it to be a lover of humanity?
What is it to love the humanity in oneself?
To embrace imperfection with positive regard
To relinquish the almost inbuilt nature to judge
Surrendering one's assumptions for connection
And accept the friction of differing beliefs

What is it to be human?
To embrace our fragility and limitations
Whilst pursuing sustainable growth
In the journey of learning to live this life well
Finding what we need in our connections
With ourselves and those close to us

What is it to be human?
To be solid in one's identity and purpose
To embrace the unanchored
And perhaps unactualized reality of your dreams
To dive headfirst into the ocean of uncertainty
And the journey of finding success
In the full meaning of the word
All to find it is laced with failure mis-labelled

To learn it will be okay
Process turned story
Turned sweet memorial stone of one's growth
Relinquish your fears and doubts
To find yourself

The Do-Not-Forgets

Before I close my eyes, my mind wakes up
A list of jobs, prompts and do-not-forgets
Reminders of everything I need to do
Oh, don't forget this, write it down
Don't forget this, write it down
Wired, wide eyed and racing
My brain is cranking and ticking
Like a factory of machines
Lights and sounds
Although I need to shut it down
...
Why do I feel this pressure?
So tense in my chest
Why do I have this alarm?
Stop
Breathe
Converse
With Mr. Heart
What are you feeling, heart?

If you forget, you will drop the ball
And we will be judged
And that will be painful!

But I respond
It's going to be okay, heart
We are not our performance
Let go of the fear and receive love
Trust in this and rest

If You Find Yourself in Crisis

Stop
Breathe...
Validate
Your emotions

Normalise
Your humanity

Evaluate
Your opinion of how you are doing

Allow yourself to be
And find your need

Remember
It all boils down to love!
And where you are on the spectrum
Of love and fear

So, find the simple statement within
Let another come in

Receive love

For you are not only in need of it
But you are worthy of it
Permission given

What is Peace?

They say peace
Positivity affects our health
That a lack of peace is linked
To diseases and heart problems

They say peace
Positively affects our mind
And a lack of peace can lead
To fight or flight impulsive decisions

They say peace
Is freedom from disturbance
But disturbance is a part of life
And a sign that you are living it

I say we need a new definition
I think peace is a journey
Of learning when to be silent
When to reflect, and what to evaluate

I believe we need to study peace
And use it as a plumbline
To change how we think and act
Continually reshaping our norm

I believe we need to practice peace
And talk about it more
That we need to let it sink in deep
Forever deep into our core

The Path Ahead

It took me a long time to realise
The vision you get from planning
Actually lights up the path ahead
Without it, we'll never see
Where we want to go

I've stumbled on this path at times
Dropping balls like I'm learning to juggle
But this planning thing means
I get to choose when I want to juggle
Just one thing at a time

It took me a long time to realise
If I don't plan rest, it doesn't happen
I'm on the journey of finding out
What rest looks like and what drains me
And it turns out I need much more rest
Than I think is productive

It took me a long time to realise
That I've been my own bully,
An unhealthy coach and a nitpicky judge
Making a list just to nail it to my door

It took me a long time to realise
That even when there's room to grow
I can rest in the process
My value is not found
In what I can achieve

Learning Grace

I really do believe we can only love others
As much as we can receive love ourselves
That we judge others by
How much we feel judged
And this judgment is normally
Self-inflicted

That's what I've seen in myself
At times a bully
Though shifting the blame

Treat others the way you'd like to be treated
This really loses its meaning
If I don't treat myself how I'd like to be treated

I am starting to learn what it means
To be a lover of my own humanity
To become friends with the tension
Of failure and growth

To stop amongst the in-between moments
To breathe and receive
To stop the negative commentary
And love myself

I am still
Learning grace
And that is okay

Kaelan Kiernan

I currently reside in Alaska with my husband, Daniel. I am a social worker by day and a musician and writer by night. This is the first time I've ever shared my poetry and it is both exciting and terrifying!

I have been writing for as long as I can remember. Books have always been my most constant friends and writing has saved me over and over in my life. My preferred medium has always been music and lyrics, but I have recently started experimenting with poetry. I love that poetry can be anything you want it to be. Poetry is an art that makes space for anyone and everyone.

As a very curious person, I have found my faith to be one of the most difficult and rewarding journeys in my life. It has not been easy, but it has been so worth it through all the ups and downs I have experienced. I am not good with absolutes and tend to believe the grey spaces are where God is found. I hope my poetry reflects that and you, too, can explore some of the nuances of Love through these words.

Fire and Rain

You are the fire and the rain
the one I cried out to,
the one I cried out for.

You are the pain
and the healing
and heartbreak-
salve for my leaking wounds.

You are beautiful
and dangerous
and soft
and rough
and full of blurs
and staggering straightforwardness.

You hide diamonds in every corner,
under the most surprising rocks-
and I want to search forever to find them all.

You are the great paradox-
the one I crave to be near
and the one I long to flee from.
The one who saves
and the one who condemns.

Or perhaps You
are infinitely bigger-
perhaps all the light in you
destroys the darkness completely
and it is simply my blindness
that leads me astray.

I want your kindness and your defence.
When you offer both
it doesn't feel like enough of either.
I long for rugged justice
but you are a God of complexities
and annoying nuances.

I wonder
when I will learn
that I can't hide
even in the depths
as I'm gently reminded
there is too much grace
too much mercy
too much peace
and too much compassion
towards me.

Love's Garden

There is no tree of good and evil
In my chest
Tempting me to sin by feeling
Tricking me into anger
Or confusion
Or pride.
There is only my neglected heart,
And Love that sits with me,
Gathering my tears,
Bottling my laughter,
And holding my hand
As we trudge through
This overgrown garden
Of mislabelled emotions
That I've made
Into my refuge.

There is no tree of good and evil here,
No forbidden fruit,
Only me and Love
And the flowers
And the streams
And this forest
As proof
That what He creates is
Good
And eternal
And intentional
And whole.

Even In the Depths

I am a trapped bird,
Thrashing and panicked,
Trying to find my way out
Through a prayer or a plea—
Lord, will You accept me?

I've tried to escape this maze,
Imagining the Last Day,
Dead-ends of fear
and doubt
and judgment,
Of pain
And burning
And the hope of redemption.

Is this truly You?
This teaching that You are angry,
That You need to punish,
That Hell is for the Wicked
And Heaven for the Saint?

How can it be
That we are taught
We can name who will be saved,
Padded by artificial disclaimers
That You are the only judge?

Is it not written
That You are kind
Even to the wicked
And the ungrateful?

Did You not say
That You send rain
For both the fool
And the faithful?

Is it not ironic
That I automatically
Designate myself as the enlightened
And my brother as the deceived?

I am shrouded in pride,
The superiority of my offering,
Shallow as it is.
I count myself amongst the saved
Or the condemned
Depending on the day.

Are You that fickle?
Do the names in Your book
Change day to day,
As often as I think?

Do You hold the pen
With magic ink,
Flippantly editing
Our eternal destiny?
Is the descent into the fire
As quick and sure

As I imagine it to be?
Or is there something truer I have yet
To discover?

In this constant questioning
And thirst for certainty,
You are still near,
Your breath warming my ear
As you remind me—

You will always find me,
For You know me by name.
Even in the abyss,
You will wrench me
From the claws
Of the great darkness.

In my inquiry and faith,
In this open-shut case,
In my genius and lunacy,
You are there.

In these ponderings,
I recall that You've warned me
A thousand times
And You will a thousand more—
I can't escape Your presence.
You are here and there
And You will always find me.

Victoria Kuttainen

Victoria Kuttainen is a writer and an academic who lives and works on Bindal and Wulgurukaba land in Far North Queensland with her husband, three children, five chickens, two dogs, and a cat. Born in the UK and raised in Canada, she has found and made home in Australia, since 2003, although it's only in the last few years she started calling it that.

A wanderer and a walker, walking is her path to noticing and knowing, and writing is the ministry of telling the truth.

Saturday

I hated overcast days
growing up.
Fog-white glare:
the embodiment of meh.

On weekends,
They were rip-offs
Unlike weekdays,
When it's not like
You're free anyway.

You'd wake and know
Straightaway
The day was ruined
Your plans dashed
Everything soured
A stay-at-home day
Inside everything
Out of sorts,
Melancholy and sour.

A rare overcast Saturday
In the tropics
Brings me back to all this.

Like running into an old bully
From childhood,
Middle-aged, a little paunchy
His power gone to pot.

Looking this memory
Of forgotten feeling
Full in the face,
I wonder now:
What was this hold
He had over me?

It's just cloud cover
A muted kind of beauty
On a Saturday
The kind for staying home
For getting cosy
Under a duvet
And reading books.

A stranger comes toward me,
While I'm having these
Pondering thoughts.
Another walker under cloud cover
By the dam on a Saturday.

It's only when I walk on
That I realise
Something passed between us
Some flicker of mutual recognition
Some choice to keep on walking

Something passes, something passed
Something past between us
And lifts.

Growing Through Sand

This is the season
Where I get tired
Where blooming
Where I'm planted
Is a sheer will to power
Where the year presses down
Like a wall of high pressure
Humid and heavy
And I heave myself forward
Like I'm growing through sand.

This is the season where I want
To raise the white flag of surrender
Say I'm sorry, store's closed
Siesta time.
I'm pulling up stakes, tapping out
Going out of business
Pulling the roller-door down.

Each year, at this time
Heavier and harder
More hustling
Hassling and heckling
Hacking through shrinking time
As to-do lists hurtle me forward
Toward the oncoming end.

It's just that time of the year
In that time of my life
We'll get through
Like we always do
Staggering, straggling
Blind leading the blind.

It's just that time of the year
Where I'm tired.
And bedraggled.
And fraying at the ends.

And without even trying
I find myself in this season

And I groan
Even knowing

It won't be
My undoing

Just another remaking:

I've grown
And I'm growing.

I'm growing
Through sand.

His and Hers Walk

We are walking away together, exploring ground.
He takes a stick; I take my mobile phone.
'Leave that at home' he says, advice I ignore.
Its camera is a finding agent,
It helps me see beauty
Even though it weighs me down.
Bits and beeps in my pocket:
Messages from the busy world.
Zoom meeting at 10am, email reminder, texts,
'He's right,' I think. It's a tether I could do without.
But then it finds me a photo, and I focus through it.
'Look at this,' I say to him, as I snap up my photo.
'It's amazing, how these trees find any old crack to
grow out of.'
Him: 'Any old dark crack, that's what they find.
And poke in it.'
Her: 'And look at this: I love how these trees grow
around other trees like this, in an embrace.'
Him: 'Yeah, they squeeze each other out.'
Her: 'No, they support each other.'
Her: 'So what about this, this hole with a stick in it?'
Him: 'Oh, that's just a hole with a stick in it.'
We walk on.
He tells me his Theory of Karens. Mind you, this is
in response to my Theory of Karens I told him of
earlier, which he tells me is only partially right.
After a while, we stop talking.
No more beeps and bips.
We find the beauty together.
This is how we walk.

Blocked ways, Open ways

Some days are sealed off.
Like tunnelling through rock.
Not even actively spelunking:
Just knocking and scraping,
Making marks in the dark
On some doorway to nowhere
The nowhere of nope.

Some days are all watching and waiting
And nothing turns up.
No way opens up
No path finding forward
No light from above
The only signs that you read
Are signs saying no.
No trespassing here.
No entry allowed.

But some nights a spirit comes
And takes you by surprise,
You watch and see
The chest of ocean
Lift to breathe
And your daytime lightness becomes a bowsprit
Gliding over hulk.

Prayer is like this. So is writing.
Blocked ways and open ways:
There's no accounting for it.

Franki

I am barely together, yet completely whole. This is why I write. To process the parts that still feel broken. Often, I write without knowing the ending and then, as if having existed within me the entire time, I find the words. I write to learn, listening in a new way, clinging to and desperately trying to find Love in the darkest parts, sometimes having to trek right into the middle of the blackness of my inner world to find the way out. This is why I write. To find my way back to Love.

My poems are short. I like to say as much as possible with few, simple words. I write about trauma, grief, my family and faith, which has slowly been deconstructed. I am not sure if it's over yet. But I am so comfortable out here in the mystery.

This year I am releasing my first book of poems, titled How to Find Love in Dark, which is strange as I am not really a writer. I am just a person trying to heal.

On Prayer

My favourite
kind of prayer
is where I don't
speak but
lie down and
close my eyes,
having seen
yours last.

Finding My Why

I have found
my created purpose
in the knowledge
of how Love has
brought me into
itself, inviting a
curious mind
to ask of the
mysteries of
the cosmos,
of life and
love.

[A paraphrasing of
Psalms 27:4]

The Kiss

I'm tired,
the way
someone
at the end
of their life
is tired.

Lying in this bed
head under
covers,
my youngest
presses
her lips
against
my hands.

I always thought
loving others
meant emptying
oneself,
but now that
I'm empty,
I can still
love
just as
fiercely
as I did
before.

I'm still tired
but now
I know
it wasn't
love
that made
me weary.

So, I give
myself
permission
to love
and return
the kiss.

Sunday School

What happened to
all the children
from Sunday
school?

Two trees.
One garden.
All humanity and
A choice.
Good or Evil.
I must ask.
Wasn't there
another tree?
Or was our
only fate
to make a life
out here, in the
dry fields
beyond
the garden
gates?
Singing our
hallelujah
to the dust?

To a God that was
all loving, yet
hated our
humanity?
Paint blood over
the doors, lest
death take us out.
Ask for forgiveness.
Rinse, repent
and repeat.
God had
such a big plan
for you, son.
Let's pray
the prayer again.
Lest death take
you out.

What happened to
all the children from
Sunday school?
What happened
to their hallelujah?
Why did they stop
singing, out here
in the dust?

Jessica Mussro

I'm a hybrid of Italian immigrants and Tennessee moonshiners living next to the ancient Blue Ridge mountains. I moved frequently growing up, changing states or countries every several years until I was eighteen. Fortunately, the world of words—stories, books, imagination—created a haven undisturbed by packing paper and suitcases.

These days, poetry fills a space that other writing cannot. Poetry calls me to attention: to questions, to the spaces between words and emotions, to the tiny happenings in my environment. In those places, the Divine is usually waiting for me.

Studying and working in international contexts also teaches me to pay attention. As I interact with new cultural or individual ways of being, I'm prompted to make more room in my thinking and writing.

The Oldest Mountains

First, youth's unconscious optimism—
sheer ambition and pluck raise
craggy arms to show what they can do.
They are the champions
all steep awareness, all extremes
naked and unashamed.

Under millennial caresses
rock gives way before slow questioning:
how much life can you hold?

In the end, shrunken hills roll
in green and creeping arms,
tumbled stones are homes for smaller things
with nothing left to prove
and everything to offer.

Hearing an Interview with Matthew Sanford

the body is always faithful to living.
whatever is encountered
    or made
whatever festers unseen,

the body responds with strategies
for new beginnings,
    reaching toward what is alive.

the world's deep current
hums to us
beneath bone and dark
    waters
our slender filament answers
    flickers, sings
always
always choosing life.

The Swifts

then the swifts fell on the lake
all together
a hundred
tiny bodies gyring, a cyclone
skimming water
hunger and glee

like children they return
and return
    unwearied
as if every morning's delight is essential
and necessity is the mother of abandon

Mary of Bethany

My mother, grandmother, aunts
saved for years
bargained and harassed a dozen merchants
for this fragrance
then hid it away, beyond my reach
even for a reverent sniff.
"For your wedding," they told me again and again
"This is your future" much discussed over
and over cups of grape wine and sage tea
greying heads with sly smiles—
This is what love will smell like when it finds you.

That's how I recognized him.

Through slow years their voices hushed
and my father died, too.
Love might have found me earlier, but I was busy
with grief
and staying alive.

He drew me beyond survival.

I had nothing to give him
besides
this expired future, its translucent box.

He is in the Field

Spring in the hills can go to your head.
Dense green shoots fill the animals' mouths and root in
your brain.
Raw heat floods the days with queer energy:
to leap
the rocks,
shout at David's tired village, to want
a woman beside you
instead of the new lambs.

Nights are cold.
Sheep start and wander at midnight noises
at skies split with fearsome songs.
You cower, too, against the light and voices
but you go to obey—
at least, to see how far
the delusion will take
you.

To a home, its animals.
Two drawn, sweating faces bent above one small
and wrinkled
to new-lamb scent:
afterbirth, grass, milk, dung.

Unto you is born: the grass
animals
a frail, perfect hand.

This will be a sign: he will smell like you.

You watch him touch the straw, his mother's hair
you look away and try to pray.

You watch him and try to pray.

You wonder if you're praying to
him, to God
or the stars
making these ugly rocks
sing.

Jessica Stevens

I grew up in a small country town in New South Wales, Australia – this is where I developed the foundations of love for country, living off the land, bush walking and camping adventures, witnessing the spirit of community and a sense of belonging.

My twenties played a pinnacle role in my life, where I hit the ground running and found my entrepreneur feet, travelled the world, got married, and had children. Life was good, or so I thought.

I found, in my thirties, burnout knocking on my door and made itself at home for a short while. I decided to walk away from it all. The children and I relocated to start a new life.

As life slowed down its pace, I was able to enjoy life through various hobbies and took up creative writing as a means of healing and self-expression.

You can find out more about me at https://jessicajstevens.wixsite.com or find me on various social media platforms.

The Secret

It's been two years...
Since I said no more,
I deserve better than this
and ended my marriage of seven years.

It's been two years...
Since my happily ever after
came crashing all around me.

It's been two years...
Since letting go of the hopes & dreams I had for us
as a couple, and as a family

It's been two years...
Since everything in my world changed;
not one thing in my life remained the same.

It's been two years...
Since moving towards the unknown,
rebuilding the life I've always wanted.

It's been two years...
Since I began my healing journey;
learning to love myself,
forgive myself & others.
Learning to live with purpose.

It's been two years...
I now have that freeing feeling
of being able to say,

"that's not me anymore"

as I look back on the past
and acknowledge where I was
and where I am heading.

It's been two years...
So today,
I close my eyes to old ends
And open my heart to new beginnings.

Today...
The secret for my happiness is freedom,
the secret for my freedom is courage.

People You Meet

In life, you will realise there is a role for everyone you meet. Some will test you; some will use you; some will genuinely love you and some will teach you.

But those who are truly important are the ones who bring out the best in you. They are the rare and amazing people who remind you why it's worth it

You don't meet people by chance.

Self-Love

Ocean blue,
Wash away the hue,
In which I have submerged.

Dime a dozen,
In which one is rare,
Real, vulnerable & true.
My mind,
My heart,
My soul,
My body,
Open and bare
...seeking a reciprocal love to share.

To only find,
            the seeking is,
                        within

Resolve

I've been running to keep up the pace,
The expectations of other's timeframes.
Their perception of my healing, my grieving,
my evolving.

To rebuild, rediscover, restore,
in which I've had to face...alone.
One in which, you cannot be looking
at the clock,
but to dive deeper,
beneath the surface.

To feel what I feel.
Avoidance in becoming numb
and suppress what arises.
Lean into it, all of it.

Healing isn't a race.
But a journey, only for you to understand.
Only for you to conquer.
Even when you don't know the answers
or the destination.
You're learning to understand you.

The more you lean into the healing,
the more you resolve...
Resolve the grief.
Resolve the fear,

Resolve the forever-connecting-everything,
to why you do what you do,
why you think, believe, feel, react and respond to...
in the resolving lies the unfolding

Letting go of ego, the numbness,
and embracing the new.
The more clarity, joy and peace I have found
...all in my time. When I am ready

Learning to break free from the shackles
that once held me back-
the masks I felt I needed to wear to fulfil others'
perceptions and expectations of me.

The familiarity and comfort are a distant memory.
You are becoming beautifully aware of you.
Your desires,
Your beliefs,
Your purpose,
Your dreams...all things, that make you, You!

Your sense of belonging,
being welcomed with open arms.
You're lovingly coming home to yourself.

A new, bright and wonderful future is near.
It. Is. Here.

Nicole Walker

I grew up on farms in Queensland, a childhood that allowed me to roam free and indulge my lifelong love of horses.

I came to faith as a teenager in the 80s in a youth group in a small country town and it is a faith that has sustained me ever since. My greatest joy (and challenge) is parenting my three children. After much travelling and adventuring, several degrees and professions, experiencing love, loss, trauma and all the questioning that brings, I am heeding the call to a simpler life. I hope it is a life that speaks of care and connection, faith, friendship, ponies, a love of reading, writing, and finding joy and rest in small things.

Being part of this Poetry Collective has been a wonderfully affirming journey of writing and listening and learning.

My poems, I hope, reflect my desire to see the beauty and challenge of life in the absolutely ordinary every day.

I can be found on Instagram: @nicolewalker_1

The Call

In the steadfastness of grey gums
and in the shadowed skies of untamed spaces;
in following winding paths on sacred ground
and in the song of the magpie's wing;
in the open-handed ruffling of fur
and the gathering of remnant feathers -
there is the call to solace
   and ease
        and soul deep breathing.

When contained for too long,
when cornered or controlled,
I listen for
the call of the wild things,
the call to reclaim rest
the call to come back to my heart,
     the wild thing
       that barefoot breathes peace.

The Greeting

In an early morning dense with mist and silence,
hoof falls on dew damp ground herald the arrival of
a bay coated mare.
She has sensed my arrival.
Deliberate in her intent to greet,
her outstretched whiskered muzzle
softly breathes warmth into my hand.

A momentary meeting of hand and heart.

I savor the trust,
that she should grant me worthy of the greeting.
Her nuzzling question – What brings you here?
This does –
    this communion of two early morning souls.

Lantana

I would like to lay my griefs out like a well curated and
ordered garden bed,
the landscape plotted and pieced – fold, fallow, and
plough;
Neatly constrained and bordered,
Maintained by careful pruning and tended so that
(according to 'Insta' wellness advice)
they blossom into new growth, bear new fruit - the
reward for neat control.

But,
They refuse to be thus tamed.
Lantana like, they cling to memory, weaving sorrow
into love.

Only You Know

I am the
Dry Bones
cleaved to the dust,
stripped of dreams
by winds whirling
with loss and betrayal.
I am the
Dry Bones
powerless,
exposed,
in valleys
of grief and unknowing.
Can these bones live again?

Sovereign Lord, only you know.

This is the hope I hear:
We are the bones of the Earth
and you are our God.
An absurd hope in One who knows and sees beyond.
A brave beautiful hope in the uncertainty.
Only You know.

Friendship

When I was fading away,
fragile
and diminished
and weary,
 I looked to you, my friend
And you refused the fading.

You were the custodian
of a kaleidoscope of memories woven over time:
that spoke of love
and hope
and the belief in new beginnings
And they refused the fading.

And I saw myself reflected in your eyes
in glorious hopeful technicolor.
And I refused the fading.
I refused the fading.

I Have a Friend in Anger
(FOR SUE)

When the tentacles of anger first reached through her,
they had been unwelcome,
a shameful sign:
of spiritual immaturity,
of a lack of self-control,
of her inability to make him happy.

But shame had lied: anger was her friend

Anger, first politely applied as a full stop, completing
the words spoken of what she was not.
Anger, quietly growing, fertilized by ignored pleas for
change.
Anger, uncoiling and spreading, lashing and railing, its
dark strength flowing protection around her heart and
lifting, stripping away blinkered beliefs about love and
sacrifice.
Anger, giving volume to the scream –
Stop. No. More. You. Will. Do. This. No. More.
Anger, slashing and burning, to lay waste to the lies, to
clear the way forward.

Oh, what a friend she had in anger.

Tineke Ziemer

Who am I? That's a question I find hard to answer these days. In the past, these labels would have rolled easily off my tongue: Christian, church-leader's kid, wife of twenty years, home-schooling mom, homeowner, and the favourite of our delightful golden retriever. In one year, all those titles were swept off the table and I am just beginning to assemble the broken pieces of my identity into something new and beautiful.

When this collective began, it found me living alone in my rural hometown in British Columbia, Canada. Since then, I have spread my wings and relocated temporarily to the beachside city of Troon in Scotland. I've always found healing through creative expression, so it was natural to turn to poetry during this transition. Solace has also come through my career as a professional photographer, which has been funding my love of travel and adventure for over twenty years.

I have always found my value in achievements, but my past successes seem to have little meaning now. Instead, the greatest discovery of my life has been the unveiling of Measureless Love – a Love that knows no separation, no shame and no harm. Some refer to this Love as God; I simply say "Friend."

Loved – that's who I am.

Grief Echoes

Grief echoes
like the sharp crack of an ancient cedar
giving way to death
    Falling
        Falling
          Falling
until earth and body violently connect,
breaking the stillness of the forest,
with a final s-h-u-d-d-e-r-i-n-g breath

And
all
is
still.

There her corpse wastes and withers,
giving shelter to woodland critters,
no distinction for saint or sinner
all may find asylum within her

There her carcass resting remains,
enriching the soil with her decay,
still sharing in death her earthen grave
with souls who've yet to come awake

Sky sighs
like the whisper of an ancient keeper
releasing the winged seed to glide
      Floating
          Floating
             Floating
until spore and fertile womb collide
conceiving from union of life and death
a descendant to nurse at mother earth's breast

And
all
is
well.

For
Grief echoes
      echoes
         echoes
yet joy...
joy--
Joy!

It grows.

Love Finds a Way

How do I grieve someone
when I only
ever knew
the person
I wished they were?

Who am I bidding farewell to
but a projection of myself?
A conjuring of my own will?
A desperate attempt
to manifest
my own purity
in the heart of another?

In that case,
best not to say goodbye at all
but rather
give a warm welcome
to the scattered parts of my self
who were
loving me
vicariously
through a stranger
all along.

Jump

There's a fine line between courage and crazy.
Will it all turn out? I dunno, maybe.

I could ask myself: What if?
What will they think? How will I choose?
But I'd rather say: Why not?
Who cares? What do I have to lose?

If all my friends jumped off a cliff,
would I jump too?
Heck no! I'd be first in line
to take the plunge! Wouldn't you?

You may look at my life
and be full of envy
but we all have the same choice
to make eventually,
to say yes to adventure
or to idolize certainty.

It's a no brainer!
We're all living on borrowed time.
Guarantees are an illusion
so I've kissed sanity goodbye.
In the end I'd rather be crazy
if it gives me the courage to fly.

Letting Go and Finding

I wonder why I always felt
the heaviness of your happiness?
Why did I carry your weight
on my tiny shoulders?
If you're happy, I'm happy ... or so I thought.

A little girl could never anticipate
all the ways you'd find
to be dissatisfied
or all the scriptures
you'd never hesitate to use
as weapons of mass destruction.

A child could never predict
that the only way
to remain in your love
was to disappear all together
and cease to e x i s t at all.

Follow in daddy's footsteps, they said.
So, I tried to bleed out
all that wasn't right
by cutting my own flesh
but little did I know
you'd take it one step further
by cutting out your own flesh
and blood
and throwing me   away.

A daughter of God,
made in His image,
can't know her Father
when her father
has made god in his own image
and is not conformed to this world
but is transformed by the closing
of his mind.

What does your dad think? they ask.
Which dad? I wonder.
You? Who lives by the law
of stepping away
or the stepdads who have
stepped up
   stepped forward
      and walked each step
            by my side?

I wonder why
it took half a lifetime
for me to let go
and let you go
and go
to a Father's lap
who loves.
And loves
And loves.
And loves.

Do you want to be part of a future
Poetry Chapel Book,
writing alongside David Tensen?

You could be in the next collective;
writings, sharing, healing and learning through
poetry and publishing.

Limited spots per intake.

Visit www.davidtensen.com/poetrychapel
for more information.

THE SAVING I NEED

available in eBook and Audiobook format.

Also by David Tensen:

The Wrestle

Poems of divine disappointment and discovery.

2020

So I Wrote You A Poem

Poems of empathy on life, loss and faith.

2021

Support the author by purchasing via

www.davidtensen.com

e: david@davidtensen.com

ig: @david_tensen
fb: /davidtensenwriter
tw: @davidtensen

About the Author & Editor

Australian poet David Tensen brings form and beauty to our deep spiritual yearnings. Drawing from decades of experience in pastoral care, leadership and spiritual development, his poems have found their way into hearts of many. Raw, accessible, and prophetic, David's writings uncover pain and bring healing to it.

David, his wife Natalie, and three children live in Queensland, Australia.